BAPTISM
THE PICTURE AND ITS PURPOSE

PETER MASTERS

SWORD & TROWEL
METROPOLITAN TABERNACLE
LONDON

BAPTISM
THE PICTURE AND ITS PURPOSE

© Peter Masters 1994

SWORD & TROWEL
Metropolitan Tabernacle
Elephant & Castle
London SE1 6SD
ISBN 1 899046 01 1

Cover design by Andrew Sides

All rights reserved. No part of this publication may be reproduced or transmitted in any form or by any means, electronic or mechanical, including photocopy, recording, or any information storage and retrieval system, without permission in writing from the publisher.

Printed in Great Britain by Bocardo Press, Hawksworth, Didcot, Oxon

Baptism
The Picture and its Purpose

Go ye therefore, and teach all nations, baptising them in the name of the Father, and of the Son, and of the Holy Ghost (Matthew 28.19). Repent, and be baptised every one of you (Acts 2.38).

WE FIND IN THE New Testament an inseparable link between conversion and baptism. In character, the two are poles apart. Conversion is spiritual; whereas baptism is merely physical. Conversion is a new birth imparted from above; while baptism is carried out by a pastor or elder of the church. Conversion is a powerful, inward, soul-renewing work. Baptism is only an outward picture, having no soul-saving power whatsoever.

Nevertheless, in the New Testament, repentance and conversion are inseparable from baptism. Conversion is the real thing – baptism is merely a picture of it; yet wherever there is a conversion, the picture must follow. *Acts 8.36* provides an example of this. The chancellor of Ethiopia believed in the Lord, and very soon asked, 'What doth hinder me to be baptised?'

Although it is true that baptism is not essential to salvation (how can it be, as it *follows* conversion?), yet it is very clearly required by the Lord

Jesus Christ, and Christian people are therefore *bound* to seek baptism in obedience to Him.

Baptism is a *Christian ordinance*, which means that it has been expressly commanded by the Lord Jesus Christ Himself. There are only two pictorially significant 'rites' to be carried out by the Christian church, and these are baptism and the Lord's Supper, both of which were especially ordained (hence called *ordinances*) by the Lord. Both are richly illustrative in character, portraying the saving work of Christ and the new spiritual relationship between Him and His people. Both are designed to bring glory and honour to Christ, and to strengthen and bless His people. It is imperative that we grasp their meaning, and honour them fully.

It is clear that in New Testament days *every* true believer willingly obeyed the Lord's command to be baptised. We would point, for example, to *1 Corinthians 12.13*, 'For by one Spirit are we all baptised into one body.' This clearly refers to physical baptism, as the commentators generally point out. Calvin says, 'Paul, of course, is speaking about the baptism of believers.' In this verse Paul is certain that all believers in fellowship with the church at Corinth had been baptised. Similarly he assumes that the Colossian members were all baptised when he says that they had been 'buried with him *[Christ]* in baptism' *(Colossians 2.12)*. Writing to the Galatians *(3.27)*, Paul equates all who had been baptised with those who had 'put on Christ'. In other words, all converts were baptised.

The helpfulness of baptism

The great question for us is – Why should the Lord insist on the baptism of all converts? What is the significance of baptism? What makes it so important, especially in the light of the fact that it has no spiritual contribution to make towards conversion? The answer is that the Lord designed this ordinance to consolidate Christians in their walk, to inspire and preserve churches, and to give a clear announcement to the world about the nature of the Christian church. If it is neglected or wrongly administered, then the Lord's purposes are disregarded and obstructed by the very people who should be His loyal servants.

Before we look at the various matters so vividly illustrated in baptism, let us consider how the 'parties' just mentioned are helped.

Firstly, baptism helps individual believers to crystallise their own testimony and express it. It impresses their conversion experience upon their minds in such a way that their gratitude rises and their assurance is strengthened. Furthermore, they realise that, whereas their conversion has been an inward, unseen transaction between themselves and the Lord, it must now be expressed and lived out before the eyes of the world, and accordingly they pledge themselves to obey the Lord and to be faithful to Him in all circumstances.

Secondly, baptism helps the church, because, just as the Lord's Supper keeps *Calvary* in our view, baptism keeps *conversion* before us. We are reminded that conversion is our chief business, and that we are a 'royal priesthood' whose great objective is to 'shew forth the praises' of the Lord *(1 Peter 2.9)*, and to call men and women to Him. Every baptismal service profoundly moves the people of God, lifts our morale, and encourages us forward in the great campaign for souls. Baptism places the necessity and glory of evangelism at the forefront of the life of the church, and that is what the Lord intended.

Thirdly, baptism helps unbelievers (all those, at least, who come within the influence of a live, baptising church) because it emphasises the sharp line of distinction between saved and unsaved people. Many unconverted men and women enter our churches and hear the Gospel preached. Often we see their evident concern. But time passes, and we grow used to them, and they grow used to the Gospel, sometimes becoming permanent seekers, or nominal Christians. Then they are confronted by the testimony of those who pass through the waters of baptism – those who have clearly obeyed the call, and have found forgiveness and new life. As the glorious features of conversion are made conspicuous, the call of the Gospel often pierces the complacency of dilatory and deluded souls in a new way. 'Vague believers' see that there must be a response to the Word, and that nothing short of the new birth is genuine Christianity. The testimony of baptism speaks powerfully to these 'almost believers'.

As far as unconverted observers are concerned, baptism places a very visible 'bar' on the fellowship of the church. Baptism says that to become a member of the household of God, a member of the church, an experience of conversion is essential. It proclaims the necessity of the death of the old life, and the clear acquisition of a new life, before people may truly call themselves Christians. (It should be obvious that the practice of infant baptism contradicts this purpose, for it tells the world the very opposite, that the Christian life is entered by a religious ceremony as a baby, and not by means of a conscious conversion experience.)

There are many churches where believers are in no way distinguished from unbelievers. But where churches hold baptismal services, everyone is reminded that the church is not just a parish roll, or a company of people who merely assent to Christian teaching. Baptism declares that the church is a company of saved people, and keeps in view the distinction between spiritual death and spiritual life. It is no wonder baptism was commanded by the Lord!

Having considered some of the obvious benefits of baptism, we must look further at the matters most obviously illustrated. What does the action of baptising people in water actually picture? Four major points are to be noted in the symbolism of baptism.

BAPTISM – A FOUR-PART ILLUSTRATION
(1) Of obedience

Firstly, baptism is a picture of obedience. The call of the Lord goes out: 'Repent, and be baptised.' We obey the call to repent in the secrecy of our hearts, and then the call to be baptised is obeyed in an outward, visible way as a public demonstration of our spiritual obedience to God.

What a perfect picture baptism is of spiritual obedience! People may think, 'Why do these Christians submit to such a humbling ceremony? Why do they choose to go through this simple and inconvenient act? It allows for no individuality or freedom of expression, nor is it varied to allow for one's class or race or wealth, nor has it developed in form over the centuries. They seem to do it just because they believe that God has told them to.'

That is precisely the message of baptism. It says that God has determined the way of salvation, and it is the same for all people. It says that obedience to God's call is the only way to know Him. It says that the same humbling, unwelcome step of repentance must be taken by all – rich and poor, young and old alike.

'But,' the unbeliever may think, 'is there no flexibility? Are there not many ways to please God? Can we not make our own passage to Heaven, keeping some measure of our pride and self-determination?' No, replies the picture of baptism. There is one Gospel, and one way for all, and this must be embraced by all. To come to Christ is a matter of obeying the call to repent, to believe, and to yield to His lordship. Baptism proclaims 'obedience to the faith' as the only way to God.

(2) Of forgiveness

Secondly, baptism is clearly a picture of forgiveness, and it speaks to both believers and unbelievers, proclaiming that the washing away of sin is the vital heart of salvation. As converted believers pass through the waters of baptism, they effectively say, 'I have been *entirely* washed by the pardoning mercy of God.' So baptism conveys a picture, not of people fondly imagining that they can please God by their own efforts, but of people who admit their need of free and total pardon.

Naturally, only total immersion gives a picture of total forgiveness. What kind of picture is provided if baptism is performed by sprinkling or pouring a small amount of water upon someone? How can that portray total cleansing? Does it not suggest that only *partial* cleansing is needed; just a little measure of forgiveness; merely a little wash?

If we have received total forgiveness, then we should want our baptism to be a fitting illustration, as the Scripture requires. True baptism is an eloquent declaration that the washing away of all guilt is necessary for real conversion to God.

(3) Of new life

The third great truth illustrated by baptism is the radical change of life and character that takes place at conversion. 'If any man be in Christ,' says Paul, 'he is a new creature: old things are passed away; behold, all things are become new' *(2 Corinthians 5.17)*.

Baptism by immersion vividly illustrates this new life because it depicts the processes of burial and rising again. The apostle Paul refers to this in *Romans 6.3-4* – 'Know ye not, that so many of us as were baptised into Jesus Christ were baptised into his death? Therefore we are buried with him by baptism into death: that like as Christ was raised up from the dead by the glory of the Father, even so we also should walk in newness of life.' He died to take away my sin, and my old life has died with Him!

Paul uses similar words in *Colossians 2.12* – 'Buried with him in baptism, wherein also ye are risen with him through the faith of the operation of God.'

These passages point out that, for believers in Rome and Colosse, baptism was a picture of their new-life experience. 'Look back at your baptism,' the apostle seems to say, 'do you recall how well it demonstrated what God had done for you, and what happened to you?'

Their baptism pictured their death to their sinful past and former lifestyle. At the same time it spoke of how they were raised up (in the new birth) to live a new life. It was a picture of their having died as devotees of this world (the kingdom of darkness) and having been raised anew as members of the kingdom of God's dear Son.

Could there be a more expressive outward sign of the great transformation brought about by conversion? The believer goes down under the water to illustrate that old things are dead and past, and rises to show that all has become new. In doing this the believer expresses a fine visual testimony, the people of God rejoice, and unbelievers are moved by the Spirit to realise the true nature of conversion.

This aspect of baptism is acknowledged by the great divines of the past, even those who did not subscribe to baptism by immersion. Calvin, for example, says, 'Baptism . . . is not a washing only, but also the putting to death of the old man . . . baptism means that we die to ourselves and become new creatures.' But how can the sprinkling or pouring of water illustrate burial and resurrection? The only adequate and meaningful mode of baptism is that of immersion.

(4) Of identification with Christ

The fourth important picture presented by baptism is that of how true converts become closely identified with Christ. They now belong to Him, stand with Him, represent Him, love Him, live for Him, and they will be faithful to Him. Baptism pictures this because, in being baptised, converted people follow His example, doing exactly what He did. They track, as it were, His footsteps through the baptismal water.

In *Matthew 3.13-15* we read:– 'Then cometh Jesus from Galilee to Jordan unto John, to be baptised of him. But John forbad him, saying, I have need to be baptised of thee, and comest thou to me? And Jesus answering said unto him, Suffer it to be so now: for thus it becometh us to fulfil all righteousness.'

The Lord Jesus Christ had no sin and did not need to be baptised as a sign of His own repentance. What, then, was the purpose of His baptism? He tells us that it was essential for Him to fulfil all that was required of Him. *Hebrews 2.17* holds the key: 'Wherefore in all things it behoved him to be made like unto his brethren, that he might be a merciful and faithful high priest.'

It was essential for Christ to be baptised in order that His life and example should be perfect in every way, and then on Calvary He would be perfectly qualified to atone for human sin. Remember that He was appointed to be the Saviour and leader of His redeemed people. He was to be their great high priest, their forerunner, and their 'elder brother'. To fulfil these offices and tasks perfectly, it was necessary for Him to do everything that He required of His people, otherwise how could He be their forerunner and example? The captain, in the armies of old, went first, at the head of the column. He went first along all paths, and through all dangers. And Christ is the captain of our salvation *(Hebrews 2.10)*.

To fail as a perfect leader and example would tarnish the qualification of our dear Saviour to be the *perfect* sacrificial lamb. But 'in all things' He fulfilled the duties which He required of His people, and so He led the way through the waters of baptism. He identified with us, as our leader, and in baptism we tell the world that we are now identified with Him.

Can any born-again believer hold back from baptism, when the Lamb of God led the way? In baptism we say to Him, to the church, and to the outsider – 'I will follow my Saviour. I will tread the pathway of Him Who loved me and gave Himself for me. I will hold fast to Him. I will "follow the Lamb whithersoever he goeth" ' *(Revelation 14.4)*. And because immersion involves us getting into the water, and going 'through' it, it is a fitting picture of *following* the Saviour into the calling and duties of the Christian life.

Baptism, then, is a wonderful expression of our solidarity with Christ, and with all His interests. And at the same time, it is our way of identifying with the rest of God's people who have taken the same pathway – 'For by one Spirit are we all baptised into one body.'

The message of the method

The complete message presented by baptism is:

(i) A picture of obedience (in which we obey Christ's command).

(ii) A picture of forgiveness (in which immersion in water illustrates the washing away of the whole body of sin).

(iii) A picture of new life (in which the imagery of burial and rising again illustrates the radical change of having died to the old life, to receive a new, converted life).

(iv) A picture of identification (in which we tread in the steps of our Saviour and forerunner to show that we are now more closely identified with Him than with anyone or anything on earth).

It cannot be too strongly emphasised that the *method* of baptism is essential to the picture. Does the quantity of water really matter? Indeed it does. Are we to say, 'Baptism is important but the picture it yields is of no importance'? Of course not. When the method is not immersion, then the picture is radically changed. In the aspects of baptism just considered, all but the first are incapable of being portrayed except by immersion.

We would not expect an artist to paint a landscape successfully with just a few drops of paint, nor can we illustrate conversion with a few drops of water. The differences between immersion and washing amount to a totally different picture. Without immersion, the ceremony loses contact with so much of its meaning and biblical purpose.

What would non-Baptist friends say to the suggestion that a fleck of flour and wine could be dusted on to someone's brow as a valid expression of the Lord's Supper? Would it be merely a question of the *quantity* of 'bread' and wine? No, it would be a matter of serious interference with the Lord's intended picture, which requires that commonplace, staple items are eaten. So it is with baptism.

We will refer later to the New Testament teaching on immersion from graphic passages such as *Romans 6.4*, and from the meaning of the Greek verb 'to dip'. But the *pictorial purpose* of baptism should settle any argument on the matter, for the New Testament teaches plainly what baptism is intended to illustrate, and there is only one method of baptism which provides that picture. If we discard immersion, vital parts of the picture (and therefore the message) are lost, namely, those that depict *total* washing, death and new life, and our following in the steps of the Lord.

Let us never forget that baptism was commanded by Christ for all His people. He does not merely *suggest* we should be baptised. Neither does He *advise* or *recommend* it. The Lord Who bled for us looks upon us with that kindness and love which is beyond all describing – and *commands* it.

Will you be baptised? Do you now see that your Saviour insists on it as a permanent message and blessing to both the church and the world?

The following pages of this booklet take a slightly more technical look at the reasons why baptism is only for believers, rather than babies, and why it should always be by immersion. The writer urges readers to study the biblical arguments presented here even if they do not have any problems with these matters, as it is so important to understand the biblical basis of everything we do.

WHY NOT INFANT BAPTISM?
Baptism is only for believers

Why do Baptists not recognise the baptism of infants as true baptism, as commanded by the Lord? The answer is that the only baptism described in the New Testament is *believer's baptism,* which presupposes that the person to be baptised has personally and consciously believed in Christ for salvation.

This is clear from the two texts at the beginning of this booklet. In the first of these – 'Go ye therefore, and *teach* all nations, baptising them . . .' *(Matthew 28.19)* – the Greek word translated *teach* literally means *make disciples of.* Making disciples is the objective, and baptising follows. It is disciples – those who follow a teacher – who are to be baptised.

The second of our starting texts also defines baptism as being a ceremony intended for believers: 'Repent, and be baptised every one of you' *(Acts 2.38).* Here, baptism follows repentance (which obviously refers to the repentance of someone who believes the Gospel).

The words of Christ recorded in *Mark 16.15-16* also make clear that baptism is only for believers. He said, 'Go ye into all the world, and preach the gospel to every creature. He that believeth and is baptised shall be saved.'

No infants baptised in the Bible

In *Galatians 3.26-27* Paul says most emphatically, 'For ye are all the children of God by faith in Christ Jesus. For as many of you as have been baptised into Christ have put on Christ.' In those days, Paul could assume that every converted person had been baptised, and every baptised person had consciously exercised faith in Christ. There were none in those days (AD 49 at the earliest) who had been baptised as infants!

All the people named in the New Testament in connection with baptism were adult believers. Not one child is mentioned. Then where does the idea come from that infants were baptised? It is simply an assumption. It has to be 'read into' the text somewhere. For example, the assumption is made that when the jailor of Philippi was baptised, his infant children were baptised with him. This is assumed because the text says that he 'was baptised, he and all his, straightway' *(Acts 16.33)*. But how do we know that he had infant children? We do not. None are mentioned. His household may have consisted only of older children and servants, a likely situation as Roman jailors were often older ex-servicemen.

However, the argument is solved for us because the previous verse says that Paul and Silas 'spake unto him the word of the Lord, and to *all that were in his house.*' In other words, they were all old enough to understand the message, and to respond to it personally. And a few verses later we read that the jailor was a rejoicing, believing man 'with *all* his house'. They were all old enough to join in the rejoicing. Without doubt, they had all believed in a conscious, personal way, and were therefore proper candidates for baptism. There were no infants in that house.

Another place where infants are assumed to be included for baptism is the very passage we referred to earlier – *Acts 2.38* – where Peter calls people to repent and be baptised, promising the gifts of the Holy Spirit to all who do so. The very next verse records that Peter said – 'For the promise is unto you, and to your children, and to all that are afar off, even as many as the Lord our God shall call.'

Does this mean that infants should be baptised, and so receive the Holy Spirit? Of course not, for the children referred to are undoubtedly the subsequent generations who will believe the message. The key words are 'even as many as the Lord our God shall call'. Whether these people are yet unborn, or living in far countries, if the call of God is heard in their hearts, and they repent of their sins, they will receive the Holy Spirit in their lives. The promise is for those who personally, consciously believe. And it is these people who are also required to testify to their salvation in baptism.

To say that infants are mentioned here as suitable candidates for baptism is to miss the clear sense of the passage, which is about how people who hear the *call* of God must *repent* in order to receive the Spirit. Tiny babies can neither hear the call nor repent, and therefore they are not in mind.

In this chapter of *Acts* the point that baptism is for believers is further reinforced in verse 41, where it is said that 'they that *gladly received his word* were baptised.' Babies cannot gladly receive the word. Luther thought that perhaps they could. He imagined that, as the minister said the words of the baptismal service, the babies could hear and understand, not with *rational* understanding (because they were too young), but with *spiritual* understanding. And Luther said that until someone could prove that this was not so, he would go on baptising babies! Few people have agreed with Luther's theory, even among the ranks of infant-baptisers.

No babies in the 'household baptisms'

Pro-infant-baptism writers flounder badly when trying to justify infant baptism from the Scripture. Even the eminent Professor Louis Berkhof in his well-loved *Systematic Theology* can suggest no biblical example of an infant being baptised, apart from a vague, hopeful reference to the texts just considered, and an equally far-fetched reference to *1 Corinthians 1.16* (where Paul says that he baptised the household of Stephanas). Prof Berkhof writes: 'The New Testament repeatedly speaks of the baptism of households, and gives no indication that this is regarded as something out of the ordinary.' However, he supplies only the two texts mentioned, and neither accommodates babies.* In the case of the household of Stephanas, Paul says in the same letter that the members of this family had 'addicted themselves to the ministry of the saints' *(1 Corinthians 16.15)*. The family was entirely devoted to the shepherding and poor relief work in the church, which proves that it was a family of adults.

The only two examples mentioned by Prof Berkhof are invalid, and all

---

* Two further texts are mentioned by other authors: the baptism of the household of Cornelius *(Acts 10.48)* and that of Lydia *(Acts 16.15)*. But the people gathered in the house of Cornelius were 'his kinsmen and near friends' who 'heard the word' *(Acts 10.24 and 44)*, not his infants, and Lydia does not appear even to have been married, for she acts as head of her house, inviting apostles to stay with her, and travelling great distances as a merchant. Her household obviously consisted of adult servants, capable of believing. Only four passages mention 'household baptism', and none of them would have involved infants.

his other arguments for infant baptism (with the exception of one, to which we will come) are embarrassingly weak. He pleads, for instance, along these lines: 'Does the Bible anywhere command the exclusion of children from baptism? Does it command that all those who are born and reared in Christian families must profess their faith before they are baptised? Clearly, there are no such commands.'

Christians should not do things in the church simply because the Bible does not exclude them. On the contrary, we should perform only those ceremonies that the Lord commands us to perform. Dr Berkhof, in common with most Presbyterians and Anglicans, attaches no importance at all to the New Testament linking of baptism with repentance. All the references to baptism insist that people *must* have a profession of their own before they may be baptised.

Is baptism equivalent to circumcision?

Another argument advanced in favour of infant baptism is along these lines: God's covenant with Abraham and his seed was a *spiritual* covenant (an 'administration' of the covenant of grace), and this covenant had a physical sign and seal of membership, namely, the circumcision of male babies. Now that the covenant is administered in a new way (through the church of Jesus Christ), the sign and seal of the covenant is baptism. And because baptism is the New Testament counterpart of circumcision, it follows that it should include the children of believers, just as circumcision did.

The first problem with accepting this idea is that we are obliged to ignore all the New Testament passages which speak of baptism as being *exclusively* a sign of repentance, faith and conversion.

Secondly, as we have noted, there is not one single example of an infant baptism in the New Testament.

But thirdly, it is simply not correct to say that baptism is the counterpart or equivalent of circumcision. This idea does not come from the Bible, and there is not a single text to support it. Nevertheless, Dr Berkhof (like most infant-baptisers) insists that it is a biblical teaching, saying, 'Baptism is substituted for circumcision, Christ clearly substituted it as such . . . *Colossians 2.11-12* clearly links up circumcision with baptism.' However, this is not so. In *Colossians 2.11-12* Paul is saying that circumcision and baptism are *not* equivalent. He is saying that physical circumcision did *not* symbolise salvation, but Christians have received *true* circumcision (deliverance from the power and dominion of sin), and this true circumcision is symbolised by baptism. In other words, baptism symbolises something far better than physical circumcision, namely, conversion.

Paul is saying that baptism is entirely different from circumcision, and far better. Circumcision reminded Jews of their special privileges in having the Word of God, special protection, and other benefits. Chiefly, it reminded people about Abraham, and how he trusted God for salvation.* But circumcision did *not* signify that they were saved simply by being born Jews! It never was a badge or sign of being one of God's ransomed, born-again people. Baptism, however, is such a sign, and therefore it is altogether different and higher than circumcision. The two must always be contrasted, and not thought of as being alike.

Because circumcision symbolised privilege, etc, and was merely a 'preaching sign' pointing to Abraham's faith (not theirs!), it was right to circumcise male babies. But because baptism signifies true conversion, it is quite improper to baptise babies.

In summary, it is vital to note that the *only* text which brings circumcision and baptism together *(Colossians 2.11-12)* presents a *contrast* between them, and not a likeness, leaving infant-baptists with no foundation at all for their belief that the one continues the job of the other. Scripture says the two are quite different.

Historically, Christians who uphold believer's baptism have usually rejected the idea that God's special relationship with the Jews in Old Testament times (the national covenant) was an 'administration' of the covenant of grace. The covenant of grace, according to Scripture,

---

* Romans 4.5, 11 show that the main purpose of circumcision was to be a sign of, or pointer to, Abraham's faith in the righteousness which God would provide for him. In other words, it was intended to remind Jews that they could not be God's people by virtue of their *race*, but only by *grace*, if they had faith like Abraham's.

embraces only true believers who trust in the righteousness provided by the Saviour, and such people cannot be lost. The Jews of the Old Testament included vast numbers of wicked and unbelieving people, including godless kings and priests. Such people showed no signs of a work of grace in their hearts, and many perished under God's hand of judgement, as a warning to others. It should be clear to us that God would never have given them circumcision as a badge or sign of grace, as if to encourage them in their presumption and wickedness.

The covenant of grace was certainly operational through the teaching of the Old Testament, but only in the lives of individuals who trusted in the mercy of God, and believed that He would provide a Saviour (just as Abraham had believed). The Jewish national covenant, which encompassed all Jews, had a different purpose from the covenant of grace, which encompasses only true believers, in every age.

THE MODE – IMMERSION
Is immersion essential?

Infant-baptists usually argue against the immersion method of baptism whether for adults or children, or they say that the method is immaterial. The light-hearted comment frequently heard from infant-baptist friends is that Baptists make 'a lot of fuss over a mere quantity of water'. If, however, baptism is a symbol or illustration designed by the Lord, then the way it is carried out is obviously of great importance. A small amount of water, as we have observed, conveys only a general idea of cleansing, and little else, so that the richness of the intended message is lost.

We should be cautioned about casual comments on the quantity of water by the words of *John 3.23:* 'And John also was baptising in Aenon near to Salim, because there was much water there.' The great John Calvin, though not a Baptist, was quite certain that this passage referred to immersion. He wrote, 'From these words it may be inferred that baptism was administered by John and Christ by plunging the whole body under water . . . Here we perceive how baptism was administered . . . for they immersed the whole body in water.'

The literal meaning of 'baptise'

The reader will probably know that the word *baptise* is not strictly an English word, but an English spelling of the Greek *baptizo*, which means *to dip entirely* (or *immerse*, or *whelm*, or *engulf*, or even *drown*). There is no dispute over the basic dictionary definition of this word. The word also means *to dye* because this was accomplished by dipping fabric into dye. Baptists have often regretted that early translators of the Bible began the tradition of not translating the Greek word into literal English, but of carrying over the Greek word itself. This course was clearly taken to avoid embarrassment to those who 'immersed' by non-immersion, such as sprinkling or pouring!

The baptism term was never used by Jews or pagan Greeks to describe their ceremonial washings. Non-immersion teachers often take the line that Christian baptism was simply an adaptation of the ceremonial washings of the Old Testament era. The Jews, for example, had a washing ceremony for a Gentile who converted to Judaism. The male convert was first circumcised and then underwent a ritual bath of purification. However, this was never called baptism. (It would surely have caused outrage if John the Baptist had hijacked and misused a 'sacred rite' of the Jewish establishment when he began to baptise!)

New Testament baptism was a brand new ceremony introduced by John the Baptist, who only baptised people who professed to believe his message, repented, and desired to make a public profession of their expectation of the Messiah. Moreover, John the Baptist never baptised babies, as far as the record shows.

W. E. Vine defines baptism as immersion (with submersion), and gives examples of how the Greeks used the baptism verb. 'Plutarchus uses it of the drawing of wine by dipping the cup into the bowl, and Plato, metaphorically, of being overwhelmed with questions.'

Even infant-baptists of the past have recognised that immersion is the meaning of the baptism word. The old *Book of Common Prayer* of the Church of England says (rather intriguingly) that the priest, in baptising a child, 'shall dip it in the water discreetly and warily . . . But if they certify that the child is weak, it shall suffice to pour water upon it.' Observing the general practice of Anglican clergy, C. H. Spurgeon commented that there were remarkable numbers of sickly children in his day. Nevertheless, the scholarly authors of the Anglican liturgy knew perfectly well that *baptizo* meant *to dip*.

One might think that the meaning of the Greek word would settle the matter in favour of immersion, and so it should. However, writers in favour of other methods are reluctant to agree that dipping is the *only* sense of the word. Prof Berkhof, for example, denies that the word has only this single sense. 'The facts,' he writes, 'as they appear in both classical and New Testament Greek, do not warrant this position.'

But when Prof Berkhof presents his 'facts' to prove that the word has an elastic meaning, we find (uncharacteristically for him) amazingly weak arguments. First, he speaks of Old Testament washings and sprinklings, providing a long list of texts, all of which are about old covenant ceremonial, and none of which uses the word *baptise*. In other words, they throw no light whatsoever on the meaning of the baptism word.

Then Prof Berkhof refers to *Mark 7.3-4*, where the *baptise* word is used in the Greek text. It is a reference to how the Jews wash or 'baptise' their hands before eating, and various other items also, including 'tables'. He exclaims: 'We cannot possibly think of dipping.' But that is precisely what they did when washing hands; they were dipped in water. And all the other items mentioned would also have been immersed in water for ceremonial washing.

Certainly, the 'tables' may appear to present a problem, but they did not have tables. The Greek word refers to *couches*, or cushions on which they reclined to eat, and these would have been draped with a piece of cloth, which was the item washed. Naturally, this would have been washed in the normal way – by immersion in water. Far from proving that 'baptism' can refer to washing by the application of water, the unvarying meaning, that of immersion, is upheld.

Prof Berkhof then lists a number of texts which speak of the baptism of the Spirit (which contain the idea of being 'overwhelmed' by the Spirit).

Despite the fact that none of these texts challenge the dictionary meaning of the baptism word *(to dip)*, Prof Berkhof draws the opposite conclusion, saying, 'Because the New Testament does not in any case explicitly assert that baptism took place by immersion, the burden of proof would seem to rest with the Baptists.'

At this point the professor appears to have forgotten that the undisputed basic meaning of *baptise* is *dip*, or *immerse*, and therefore the burden of proof rests with him to show that it could carry another meaning. This he fails to do, and yet his type of argument is generally the best that non-immersion writers can offer, for their case is unprovable.

The 'baptism' words in classical Greek

Prof Berkhof and others who take the same view often claim that in classical Greek the baptism noun and verbs are used in a wide variety of ways, including descriptions of washing and ceremonial purification. This is an appropriate point to refer to an outstanding study carried out a century ago by Professor Thomas Jefferson Conant, a leading American theologian and Bible translator (and chairman of the translation board of the American Standard Version of 1901). Prof Conant was also a noted classical scholar. In his famous study entitled *Baptizein*, he set out to locate and examine every single usage of the baptism words in Greek literature, from earliest times down to and including the New Testament, and even up to his own day. His objective was to establish once and for all whether or not this word group was ever used in any other sense than 'dipping'.

In *Baptizein*, T. J. Conant quotes *every single* instance of these words preserved in Greek literature, and finds not one example of an author deviating from the dictionary sense of 'dip-whelm-immerse-plunge'. Even the figurative, metaphorical uses of the baptism words keep to the meaning, such as when an author speaks of someone being baptised in drunkenness or debt, where the sense is obviously that of being plunged or overwhelmed, rather than that of being sprinkled or washed by the partial application of water. Never, never, never does any author depart from the one dictionary-definition sense of baptism. Non-immersion theologians ought by now to have given up their vague hope that someone, somewhere in bygone Greek literature used a baptism word to signify washing or sprinkling. The inescapable reality is that there is not one example of such elasticity of meaning either in classical or biblical Greek literature. *Baptise*, which is the Lord's term, means *dip*, and that is why we are to be baptised by immersion.

Is the burial picture intended?

We have already seen that two passages of Scripture present baptism as a picture of being buried and raised up again. Many infant-baptist teachers agree that immersion is in mind here (we have already quoted Calvin as one of these). Others, notably Professor John Murray in recent times, argue that we have no more warrant to attach to baptism the picture of burial and resurrection in these texts, than we have to attach the illustration of putting on clothing in *Galatians 3.27*. Paul, in *Galatians 3*, says, 'For as many of you as have been baptised into Christ have put on Christ' (ie: Christ's righteousness, and the 'clothing' of a new life).

However, in *Romans 6* and *Colossians 2* the symbolic association of baptism with burial and resurrection is *far too strong* to be set aside by the rather desperate tactics of evasion employed by Prof Murray! Indeed, it is so obvious that Paul intends to say that baptism pictures death and resurrection, that the overwhelming majority of infant-baptist Bible commentators agree that this is so.

It has often been pointed out that in *Galatians 3.27* Paul may have in mind the fact that immediately after baptism (by immersion) the believer puts on dry robes – a fine personal symbol of putting on Christ.

Equally, *Galatians 3.27* supports immersion from another angle, for when the believer is 'baptised *into* Christ', the process of immersion leads to that person emerging saturated or *clothed*, as it were, in Christ. In other words, immersion itself symbolises that we have 'put on' Christ in the fullest possible way. The mere application of water by sprinkling, etc, honours none of these texts. Prof Murray has only one course open to him in denying that immersion is taught in these texts – he must lamely claim that no symbolism is intended.

Infant baptism – widely differing views

The reader may not appreciate just how much division exists among infant-baptists as to what baptism means. (Infant-baptists are themselves frequently unaware that their own view is only one of several.) There are at least five major views of infant baptism, whereas there is only one view of baptism among those who hold to believer's baptism. We provide here a brief and, hopefully, not too technical survey of the different ideas of infant baptism.

Although Baptists were numerous at the time of the Reformation, the principal Reformers, sadly, held on to the Catholic practice of infant baptism, but with deep differences of opinion about its meaning. These differences were inevitable, because the baptism of babies conflicted with Reformation teaching at key points. The Reformers, for instance, emphasised justification *by faith alone*. But where was the faith of a baby?

Luther believed that a baby was regenerated – born again – through baptism, its parents expressing its faith on its behalf. (We mentioned Luther's belief earlier.) He thought that although babies did not possess *rational* understanding, they could well possess *spiritual* understanding. He admitted, however, that if it could be proved that there was no such thing as *spiritual* understanding in babies, then their baptism would be 'tomfoolery' and even 'blasphemy'.

The Lutheran approach to infant baptism was adopted by the Church of England, where the priest was commanded to say at baptism, 'This child is regenerate, and is grafted into the body of Christ . . .'

Generations of believers in the Lutheran and Anglican folds have found this kind of language very difficult to reconcile with the fact that countless baptised people do not turn out to be converted Christians. The Wesleys, for example, embraced the Church of England position that baptism gives babies spiritual life, and yet they warned multitudes *not* to depend upon their baptism as they were still children of the devil who needed to be born again.

Calvin's view was radically different from Luther's. He believed that all the children of believers were spiritually regenerate in the womb, and did not need baptism to bring this about. The purpose of baptism, for Calvin, was to serve as a sign of what had already taken place. However, it is quite obvious that not all the children of believers manifest the marks of true conversion as they proceed into childhood. Many experience conversion years later, and many not at all.

Most of Calvin's historic followers, therefore, considerably adapted his position. Some said that they only *presumed* that the child of the believer was regenerate, thus allowing for the number who would never profess Christ. (B. B. Warfield expressed this view.) Some spoke of baptism as expressing only a *promise* of salvation, and others said that the baby was not presumed to be *regenerate*, but only presumed to be *elect*. All these variants leave room for the 'real world' situation, namely, that the children do not turn out to be little Christians from birth. But the problem remains – What is the point of infant baptism?

Many infant-baptisers have not agreed with any of the positions mentioned; not that of Luther or Calvin nor any of the modifications. They say, 'We do not know what baptism signifies, and we do not think that it is important to know. We simply believe that it should be done.' Prof John Murray, for example, wrote in *Christian Baptism*, 'Why do we baptise infants? . . . It is sufficient for us to know and to answer that it is the divine institution . . . Hence to aver that baptism is dispensed to infants on the grounds of presumptive election or presumptive regeneration appears to be without warrant and also introduces perplexities into the question.'

Outstanding preachers and theologians holding to infant baptism have stumbled at the problem of showing: (i) how it is compatible with the absence of a profession of faith, and (ii) what precisely it signifies. With such diverse explanations, the infant-baptist position must be seen not as a single viewpoint, but as a cluster of quite distinct and strongly conflicting viewpoints.

The Christian who supports infant baptism will need to be able to answer the question, 'Which view or version do you believe – that of Luther, or Calvin, or one of the other distinctive views?'

SOME HISTORICAL FACTS ABOUT BAPTISTS

We are certain that the apostles of the Lord and the preachers of the early church baptised only believers, and always by immersion. Infant baptism is first mentioned in the literature of the Christian church in a treatise on baptism by Tertullian, written between AD 200 and 206. This has just a few sentences on infant baptism, and Tertullian was strongly against it. However, during the next 200 years, infant baptism became a widespread practice.

As we might expect, the original form of baptism – believer's baptism – did not die out, and history records the existence of Baptists from the first century after Christ. There is a distinctive Baptist martyrology with memorials from every century AD. (The massive volume, *Martyrs Mirror of the Defenceless Christians* compiled by Thieleman van Braght, 1660, is still published today.)

It is interesting to note that the earliest Christians in England, before the arrival of the Roman monk Augustine in AD 596, did not baptise infants. And fully-fledged Baptists were numerous in England during the twelfth century (coming from the German Waldenses). Thirty were martyred near Oxford in 1158, when Henry II had them branded on their foreheads with a red-hot iron, then whipped, stripped, and turned them out into a field in sub-zero temperatures where they died from exposure.

John Wycliffe (c1329-1384), the 'morning star of the Reformation', opposed infant baptism, and his itinerant preachers – the Lollards – were chiefly men of strong Baptist views.

At the time of the Reformation, Baptists became so numerous that Henry VIII took measures to control their growth. Latimer mentioned a town with 500 Baptists. During the reign of Edward VI they continued to grow, and during the reign of Mary, two-thirds of those burned at the stake were Baptists. During the reign of Elizabeth I, John Foxe (author of the work now known as *Foxe's Book of Martyrs*) appealed to the queen to save two Baptists condemned to death for their views, but to no avail. They perished at Smithfield in July, 1575. (The first and the last martyrs to die in England by burning at the stake were Baptists. The last was burned in 1612.)

In the history of England, Baptists more than any others have been numbered among the 'noble army of martyrs', due to their prevalence and their unswerving allegiance to the Word of God. Today, among evangelical Christians world-wide, the overwhelming majority practise believer's baptism by immersion.